30 Day Course Creation Challenge *for Authors*

Transform Your Book or Expertise into an Online Course for Your Audience!

D0902801

D'vorah Lansky, M.Ed.

An Action Guide for Authors

Vibrant Marketing Publications
Hartford, CT

Published by Vibrant Marketing Publications
Copyright ©2016 D'vorah Lansky

www.ActionGuidesForAuthors.com

ISBN 978-0-9967431-2-9

Dedication

This book is dedicated to the amazing participants in our
30 Day Course Creation Challenge for Authors program.

Your passion for sharing your message with the world is inspiring
and your dedication to helping more people,
by transforming your book, expertise, or passion
into an online course, is nothing short of amazing.

It is such an honor to be on this success journey with you!

Notes

Table of Contents and 30-Day Checklist

Notes

How to Use This Action Guide

Welcome to the 30 Day Course Creation Challenge for Authors! You have at your fingertips, a step-by-step program for creating an online course for your audience.

This action guide is divided into four parts. Each part represents an area of focus that guides you through the process of developing the foundation and content for your course. You can work on one step at a time or on multiple related steps.

While this is a 30-day challenge, you are encouraged to set the pace as it best fits with your life and your schedule. The key however, is to be consistent. While it is recommended that you go through the action steps 5-6 days a week throughout the program, your schedule may not allow for that. In that case, you may find that scheduling 3 days a week, where you focus on two action steps on each of those days, works better for you.

Here are some tips to help you make the most of this opportunity:

➤ In this guide you have access to 30 daily action steps and action pages. Go through the action steps sequentially, as they build on one another.

➤ Schedule a recurring appointment in your calendar, to go through each of the action steps. By focusing on the challenge activities at the same time each day, you'll create consistency. By treating this time as you would an appointment with your best client, you'll accomplish a great deal.

➤ When scheduling time into your calendar, select times that you'll realistically be able to dedicate to going through the action steps. This will allow you to prioritize putting the pieces in place for creating your course!

Times Scheduled in My Calendar to Focus on the Course Creation Challenge

Day of Week / Time of Day: _____

Day of Week / Time of Day: _____

Day of Week / Time of Day: _____

Have fun as you transform your book or expertise
into an online course for your audience!

Here's to Your Success!

Part One Action Steps At-A-Glance

After you complete each action step, circle back to this page and
fill in the information for your course, in the *My Course Notes* column below.
This will allow you to view your entire course, at-a-glance.

Module One: Identify Your Topic and Design Your Course	
Daily Action Step	**My Course Notes**
Day 1: Get Clear on Your "Why"	
Day 2: Identify your Target Audience	
Day 3: Identify Your Areas of Expertise	
Day 4: Decide on Your Course Topic and Title	
Day 5: Decide on Your Course Modules	
Day 6: Create Your Course Outline	
Day 7: Decide on Format for Course Content	

Part Two Action Steps At-A-Glance

After you complete each action step, circle back to this page and
fill in the information for your course, in the *My Course Notes* column.
This will allow you to view your entire course, at-a-glance.

Module Two: Develop Your Course Content	
Daily Action Step	**My Course Notes**
Day 8: Describe and Outline Module 1	
Day 9: Describe and Outline Module 2	
Day 10: Describe and Outline Module 3	
Day 11: Describe and Outline Module 4	
Day 12: Develop the Content for Module 1	
Day 13: Develop the Content for Module 2	
Day 14: Develop the Content for Module 3	
Day 15: Develop the Content for Module 4	
Day 16: Create Course Support Materials	

Part Three Action Steps At-A-Glance

After you complete each action step, circle back to this page and
fill in the information for your course, in the *My Course Notes* column below.
This will allow you to view your entire course, at-a-glance.

Module Three: Set Up Your Online Classroom	
Daily Action Step	**My Course Notes**
Day 17: Decide on Course Delivery Schedule	
Day 18: Set Up Your Online Classroom	
Day 19: Upload Your Course Content	
Day 20: Create the Sales Page for Your Course	
Day 21: Create Course Auto-Responder Series	
Day 22: Set Up a Facebook Group for Course	
Day 23: Test to Make Sure All Systems Are Go	

Part Four Action Steps At-A-Glance

After you complete each action step, circle back to this page and
fill in the information for your course, in the *My Course Notes* column.
This will allow you to view your entire course, at-a-glance.

Module Four: Market Your Course and Open the Doors	
Daily Action Step	**My Course Notes**
Day 24: Market Course via Your Email List	
Day 25: Market Course via Guest Blogging	
Day 26: Market Course via Guest Speaking	
Day 27: Market Course via Social Networks	
Day 28: Develop Joint Venture Relationships	
Day 29: Open the Doors to Your Classroom	
Day 30: Celebration and Next Steps	

Notes

Welcome To...

Part One

Identify Your Topic and Design Your Course

Day 1: Get Clear on Your "Why"

Welcome to Day 1 of the 30 Day Course Creation Challenge. Today's action step is to get clear on your "why."

Getting clear on your "why" will provide you with motivation and inspiration for creating an online course for your target audience. What is your "why" for wanting more success in your life? What is your "why" for wanting to create an online course for your audience? What will it mean to you and your audience for you to be able to achieve this goal?

Turn to *Today's Journal Page* and spend some time writing about your "why!"

Notes and Realizations

_____

_____

_____

_____

_____

_____

_____

_____

_____

_____

_____

Today's Journal Page
Get Clear on Your "Why"

What is your "why" for wanting more success in your life? _____

_____

_____

_____

What is your "why" for wanting to create an online course? _____

_____

_____

_____

How will you benefit by offering this program? _____

_____

_____

_____

How will your target audience benefit from this learning opportunity? ___

_____

_____

_____

Action Page for Day 1

Day 2: Identify Your Target Audience

Welcome to Day 2 of the 30 Day Course Creation Challenge. Today's action step is to identify your target audience.

By knowing who your target audience is, you'll be able to develop relationships with those who want and need what you have to offer. This creates a win/win situation.

Turn to *Today's Journal Page* and spend some time identifying who your target audience is. This is essential as it will allow you to maximize your efforts and your results while helping the exact people who need what you have to offer.

Notes and Realizations

_____

_____

_____

_____

_____

_____

_____

_____

_____

_____

Today's Journal Page
Identify Your Target Audience

Describe your ideal student, client, or reader: _____

_____

_____

_____

What are they most interested in?

- ○ _____
- ○ _____
- ○ _____

What are the top three things they struggle with?

- ○ _____
- ○ _____
- ○ _____

What do they most want in life?

- ○ _____
- ○ _____
- ○ _____

Action Page for Day 2

Day 3: Identify Your Areas of Expertise

Welcome to Day 3 of the 30 Day Course Creation Challenge. Today's action step is to write about your strengths and areas of expertise.

As you develop online content, you want to be clear about what it is you offer and who it is you serve. This makes for a powerful formula for success.

Turn to *Today's Journal Page* and write about your strengths and areas of expertise. Take these into account, along with the wants and needs of your target audience, as you identify possible topics for your course.

Notes and Realizations

_____

_____

_____

_____

_____

_____

_____

_____

_____

_____

Today's Journal Page
List Your Interests & Areas of Expertise

Describe your areas of expertise: _____

_____

_____

_____

_____

What interests do you have that complement your expertise?

○ _____

○ _____

○ _____

○ _____

What do you have **both** expertise in and interest in, that your audience would benefit from?

○ _____

○ _____

○ _____

○ _____

Day 4: Decide on Your Course Topic and Title

Welcome to Day 4 of the 30 Day Course Creation Challenge. Today's action step is to select the topic and title for your program.

When deciding on a title for your course, choose one that is clear and that talks about the benefit to the participant. What do your students want and what benefits will they receive as a result of participating in your program? Let this guide you as you consider a topic and title for your program.

Turn to *Today's Journal Page* and do some brainstorming on possible topics and titles for your program.

Notes and Realizations

_____

_____

_____

_____

_____

_____

_____

_____

_____

_____

Today's Journal Page
Decide on the Topic & Title for Your Program

Before selecting a topic for your course, you'll want to determine if there is an interest in that topic. Following are some exercises to help you with this.

☐ Conduct a survey of your audience to determine their interest level. You can request input from your email subscribers, social media contacts, colleagues and clients. Use SurveyMonkey.com to conduct your survey.

☐ Keep the number of survey questions to a minimum, and avoid asking for names and email addresses, as this will increase participation.

☐ Perform a keyword search, over on Amazon.com, to see if there are books and magazines related to possible topics for your course. This will indicate whether or not there is a market for these topics.

Based on your strengths, areas of expertise, and what your target audience most wants and needs, what topics would you be interested in teaching? Circle the topic you feel your audience would be **most** interested in.

○ _____

○ _____

○ _____

How will your target audience benefit from a program on this topic? _____

_____

_____

Brainstorm possible titles for your program and circle your favorite:

○ _____

○ _____

○ _____

Action Page for Day 4

Day 5: Decide on Your Course Modules

Welcome to Day 5 of the 30 Day Course Creation Challenge. Today's action step is to identify the modules you'll include in your course.

While there is no magic number for the number of modules to offer in your course, it's been found that courses of 4-5 weeks in length are long enough to provide great value and short enough to keep people involved. With this in mind, consider offering four modules in your course, as that will give you content for four sessions. If you offer sessions weekly, you'll have content for a month-long program.

Turn to *Today's Journal Page* and map out your course modules.

Notes and Realizations

_____

_____

_____

_____

_____

_____

_____

_____

_____

_____

Today's Journal Page
Decide on Your Course Modules

Refer to the brainstorm sheets on the following pages, to help you identify and narrow down the topics you'd like to include in your course.

The working title of my course is: _____

The working subtitle of my course is:_____
_____

Describe what your course will be about: _____
_____
_____
_____

What topics would you love to include in your course?

_____   _____

_____   _____

_____   _____

_____   _____

_____   _____

Decide on the four modules for your course:

○ _____

○ _____

○ _____

○ _____

Action Page for Day 5

Brainstorm List: Possible Topics for Your Course

➤ To help you identify the four modules for your course, begin by brainstorming a list of topics you'd like to teach in your course.

➤ Next, place items that are related to one another, in the boxes on the following page. You may find that your course calls for more than four modules. If that's the case, proceed accordingly. If at all posssible try to keep your course to 4-5 modules.

➤ You may not be able to fit everything on your list into your course, thats's okay. You can always offer bonus content, or save ideas for future courses.

_____ _____

_____ _____

_____ _____

_____ _____

_____ _____

_____ _____

_____ _____

_____ _____

_____ _____

_____ _____

List Related Items Together

Draw from the list on the previous page and place items in boxes that are related to one another. In this way you'll be able to identify your module topics as well as the sections of your modules.

Module One Topic:	Module Two Topic:

Module Three Topic:	Module Four Topic:

Day 6: Create Your Course Outline

Welcome to Day 6 of the 30 Day Course Creation Challenge. Today's action step is to outline the modules for your program.

Identify three key concepts that you'd like to teach in each module. You'll be able to draw from this outline, when we focus on mapping out the content for each of your modules. At that time, you'll be able to expand on the three key concepts you've listed for each module.

Turn to *Today's Journal Page* and create an outline for your course.

Notes and Realizations

_____

_____

_____

_____

_____

_____

_____

_____

_____

Today's Journal Page
Create Your Course Outline

Module 1 Title: _____

What key concepts will you teach in this module?

- ○ _____
- ○ _____
- ○ _____

Module 2 Title: _____

What key concepts will you teach in this module?

- ○ _____
- ○ _____
- ○ _____

Module 3 Title: _____

What key concepts will you teach in this module?

- ○ _____
- ○ _____
- ○ _____

Module 4 Title: _____

What key concepts will you teach in this module?

- ○ _____
- ○ _____
- ○ _____

Action Page for Day 6

Day 7: Decide on Format for Course Content

Welcome to Day 7 of the 30 Day Course Creation Challenge. Today's action step is to decide on the format for your course content.

The most popular options are:
- An eCourse delivered via email and/or your website
- A PDF Action Guide which includes training and action pages
- Audio training along with action pages
- PowerPoint Slides delivered as PDFs to accompany an audio training
- PowerPoint Slides delivered via a webinar or recorded video

Turn to *Today's Journal Page* and do some brainstorming as to which format you'd like use for your course content.

Notes and Realizations

_____

_____

_____

_____

_____

_____

_____

_____

_____

_____

Today's Journal Page
Deciding On Your Course Content Format

As you prepare to create your course, it is important to know what format you will use for delivering your course content. Complete this worksheet to help you decide on the format you'll use to deliver your course content.

Which option appeals to you most?

☐ I would like for my course to be delivered via email

☐ I'd like for my course to appear on my website or online classroom. I may write out lessons on the site, or I may provide PDF action guides.

☐ I'd like for my students to hear my voice by delivering audio content. I'd prefer the technology piece be as simple & affordable as possible.

☐ I am comfortable with online technology and would love to create a video based course.

Based on your selection above, describe what you visualize in regards to the format of your course content. You can of course create a combination course, but begin by listing the choice above that best describes your preference, and expand from there.

_____

_____

_____

_____

_____

_____

Notes

Welcome To...

Part Two

Develop Your Course Content

Day 8: Describe and Outline Module One

Welcome to Day 8 of the 30 Day Course Creation Challenge. Today's action step is to describe and create an outline for module one of your course.

Turn to *Today's Journal Page* and describe what you want your students to learn in this module. Then compose a list of action steps you'd like for them to take after completing this module.

Next, create an outline of the 3-4 key sections you'd like to teach in this module and give each section a title. These sections will form the framework for you to build this module's content around.

Notes and Realizations

_____

_____

_____

_____

_____

_____

_____

_____

_____

_____

Today's Journal Page
Describe and Outline Module #___

Module Title: _____

Describe what your students will learn in this module: _____

_____

_____

_____

_____

What action steps do you want students to take at the end of this module?

○ _____

○ _____

○ _____

○ _____

Create an outline by listing the 3-4 key concepts you would like to teach in this module? These concepts will become the sections of this module and will form the framework for you to build this module's content around.

○ _____

○ _____

○ _____

○ _____

Action Page for Day 8

Day 9: Describe and Outline Module Two

Welcome to Day 9 of the 30 Day Course Creation Challenge. Today's action step is to describe and create an outline for module two of your course.

Turn to *Today's Journal Page* and describe what you want your students to learn in this module. Then compose a list of action steps you'd like for them to take after completing this module.

Next, create an outline of the 3-4 key sections you'd like to teach in this module and give each section a title. These sections will form the framework for you to build this module's content around.

Notes and Realizations

_____

_____

_____

_____

_____

_____

_____

_____

_____

_____

Today's Journal Page
Describe and Outline Module #____

Module Title: _____

Describe what your students will learn in this module: _____

_____

_____

_____

_____

What action steps do you want students to take at the end of this module?

○ _____

○ _____

○ _____

○ _____

Create an outline by listing the 3-4 key concepts you would like to teach in this module? These concepts will become the sections of this module and will form the framework for you to build this module's content around.

○ _____

○ _____

○ _____

○ _____

Action Page for Day 9

Day 10: Describe and Outline Module Three

Welcome to Day 10 of the 30 Day Course Creation Challenge. Today's action step is to describe and create an outline for module three of your course.

Turn to *Today's Journal Page* and describe what you want your students to learn in this module. Then compose a list of action steps you'd like for them to take after completing this module.

Next, create an outline of the 3-4 key sections you'd like to teach in this module and give each section a title. These sections will form the framework for you to build this module's content around.

Notes and Realizations

_____

_____

_____

_____

_____

_____

_____

_____

_____

_____

Today's Journal Page
Describe and Outline Module #_____

Module Title: _____

Describe what your students will learn in this module: _____

_____

_____

_____

_____

What action steps do you want students to take at the end of this module?

○ _____

○ _____

○ _____

○ _____

Create an outline by listing the 3-4 key concepts you would like to teach in this module? These concepts will become the sections of this module and will form the framework for you to build this module's content around.

○ _____

○ _____

○ _____

○ _____

Action Page for Day 10

Day 11: Describe and Outline Module Four

Welcome to Day 11 of the 30 Day Course Creation Challenge. Today's action step is to describe and create an outline for module four of your course.

Turn to *Today's Journal Page* and describe what you want your students to learn in this module. Then compose a list of action steps you'd like for them to take after completing this module.

Next, create an outline of the 3-4 key sections you'd like to teach in this module and give each section a title. These sections will form the framework for you to build this module's content around.

Note: Turn the page for the *Course Outline Master for Additional* Modules.

Notes and Realizations

_____

_____

_____

_____

_____

_____

_____

_____

_____

_____

_____

Today's Journal Page
Describe and Outline Module #___

Module Title: _____

Describe what your students will learn in this module: _____

_____

_____

_____

_____

What action steps do you want students to take at the end of this module?

○ _____

○ _____

○ _____

○ _____

Create an outline by listing the 3-4 key concepts you would like to teach in this module? These concepts will become the sections of this module and will form the framework for you to build this module's content around.

○ _____

○ _____

○ _____

○ _____

Action Page for Day 11

Course Outline Master for Additional Modules
Describe and Outline Module #____

Make a copy of this master module planner, for additional or future modules.

Module Title: _____

Describe what your students will learn in this module: _____

_____

_____

_____

_____

What action steps do you want students to take at the end of this module?

○ _____

○ _____

○ _____

○ _____

Create an outline by listing the 3-4 key concepts you would like to teach in this module? These concepts will become the sections of this module and will form the framework for you to build this module's content around.

○ _____

○ _____

○ _____

○ _____

Course Outline Master for Additional Modules

Course Outline Master for Additional Modules
Describe and Outline Module #____

Make a copy of this master module planner, for additional or future modules.

Module Title: _____

Describe what your students will learn in this module: _____

_____

_____

_____

_____

What action steps do you want students to take at the end of this module?

○ _____

○ _____

○ _____

○ _____

Create an outline by listing the 3-4 key concepts you would like to teach in this module? These concepts will become the sections of this module and will form the framework for you to build this module's content around.

○ _____

○ _____

○ _____

○ _____

Course Outline Master for Additional Modules 41

Day 12: Develop the Content for Module One

Welcome to Day 12 of the 30 Day Course Creation Challenge. Today's action step is to create content for module one. You can deliver content in PDF format alone or along with audio content, via a teleseminar call.

Here are some options to chose from:

➤ Add section titles & corresponding bullet points to PowerPoint slides.

➤ Or copy and paste section titles and their corresponding bullet points into a Word document and save in PDF format.

➤ From there, you can add images and/or additional content as needed.

Turn to *Today's Journal Page* and title this module's section concepts.

Notes and Ideas

_____

_____

_____

_____

_____

_____

_____

_____

_____

Today's Journal Page
Develop the Content for Module #____

List the Key Concepts You'd Like to Teach in This Module.

Turn back to the outline you created for this module and transfer the key concepts you listed, in the spaces below.

○ _____

○ _____

○ _____

○ _____

Compose Section Titles for This Module

Now transform those concepts into benefit driven section titles. Focus on what students will gain by going through each section.

○ _____

○ _____

○ _____

○ _____

Tips for Expanding Section Titles into Course Content

Turn the page for additional exercises to help you develop the content for your course modules. The easiest way to create course content is to:

- Transfer your section titles and bullet points to PowerPoint slides or to blank pages of a Word document.

- You can then add images and expand the content from there.

Action Page for Day 12

Develop Course Content for Module #____

In the spaces below, list your module *Section Titles* for this module, from the previous page. Then compose a list of bullet points you'll cover in each of these sections. You can transfer this content to PowerPoint slides or add each section to a blank page of a Word document and expand the content from there.

Section Title: _____

- ○ _____
- ○ _____
- ○ _____

Section Title: _____

- ○ _____
- ○ _____
- ○ _____

Section Title: _____

- ○ _____
- ○ _____
- ○ _____

Section Title: _____

- ○ _____
- ○ _____
- ○ _____

Create Course Content Using PowerPoint Slides

PowerPoint is a fantastic tool for creating your course content. It is simple to use and it is easy to add text and images. PowerPoint slides, saved in PDF format, can stand alone as module content, or can complement a tele-seminar type conference call.

Tips for Creating PowerPoint Slides for Your Modules

➤ You never want to give students your PowerPoint slides. Instead, you can save 3 slides to a page with room for notes, and save as a PDF file.

➤ When creating slides, realize that less is more and images are great.

➤ Use minimal text and add no more than 3-4 bullets per slide.

➤ Make sure your text is visible by using 28-32 point font.

➤ Add images as this will keep your audience engaged. Make sure you have the rights to use these images. You can purchase them for about a dollar each at places like Fotolia.com and you can get them for free at public domain websites such as Pixabay.com

Suggestions for Which Slides to Include in Your Module

- Welcome to (Course Name) - The focus of today's module is...
- What We'll Cover in this Module. Add bullet points.
- Section Title Slides. Add a section title slide for each section of the module. On these slides list the bullet points from the previous page.
- You can then add 1-3 slides after each section title slide, and fill in the content (text and images) from there.
- Time to Take Action. Provide students with 3-5 simple action steps.

An Alternative to PowerPoint is to Use a Program Such as Word

- Copy and paste section titles and their corresponding bullet points to blank pages of a Word document.
- Add images and expand on the content & save in PDF format.

Day 13: Develop the Content for Module Two

Welcome to Day 13 of the 30 Day Course Creation Challenge. Today's action step is to create content for module two. You can deliver content in PDF format alone or along with audio content, via a teleseminar call.

Here are some options to chose from:

➤ Add section titles & corresponding bullet points to PowerPoint slides.

➤ Or copy and paste section titles and their corresponding bullet points into a Word document and save in PDF format.

➤ From there, you can add images and/or additional content as needed.

Turn to *Today's Journal Page* and title this module's section concepts.

Notes and Ideas

_____

_____

_____

_____

_____

_____

_____

_____

_____

Today's Journal Page
Develop the Content for Module #___

List the Key Concepts You'd Like to Teach in This Module.

Turn back to the outline you created for this module and transfer the key concepts you listed, in the spaces below.

○ _____

○ _____

○ _____

○ _____

Compose Section Titles for This Module

Now transform those concepts into benefit driven section titles. Focus on what students will gain by going through each section.

○ _____

○ _____

○ _____

○ _____

Tips for Expanding Section Titles into Course Content

Turn the page for additional exercises to help you develop the content for your course modules. The easiest way to create course content is to:

- Transfer your section titles and bullet points to PowerPoint slides or to blank pages of a Word document.

- You can then add images and expand the content from there.

Action Page for Day 13

Develop Course Content for Module #___

In the spaces below, list your module *Section Titles* for this module, from the previous page. Then compose a list of bullet points you'll cover in each of these sections. You can transfer this content to PowerPoint slides or add each section to a blank page of a Word document and expand the content from there.

Section Title: _____

- ○ _____
- ○ _____
- ○ _____

Section Title: _____

- ○ _____
- ○ _____
- ○ _____

Section Title: _____

- ○ _____
- ○ _____
- ○ _____

Section Title: _____

- ○ _____
- ○ _____
- ○ _____

Create Course Content Using PowerPoint Slides

PowerPoint is a fantastic tool for creating your course content. It is simple to use and it is easy to add text and images. PowerPoint slides, saved in PDF format, can stand alone as module content, or can complement a tele-seminar type conference call.

Tips for Creating PowerPoint Slides for Your Modules

➤ You never want to give students your PowerPoint slides. Instead, you can save 3 slides to a page with room for notes, and save as a PDF file.

➤ When creating slides, realize that less is more and images are great.

➤ Use minimal text and add no more than 3-4 bullets per slide.

➤ Make sure your text is visible by using 28-32 point font.

➤ Add images as this will keep your audience engaged. Make sure you have the rights to use these images. You can purchase them for about a dollar each at places like Fotolia.com and you can get them for free at public domain websites such as Pixabay.com

Suggestions for Which Slides to Include in Your Module

- Welcome to (Course Name) - The focus of today's module is...
- What We'll Cover in this Module. Add bullet points.
- Section Title Slides. Add a section title slide for each section of the module. On these slides list the bullet points from the previous page.
- You can then add 1-3 slides after each section title slide, and fill in the content (text and images) from there.
- Time to Take Action. Provide students with 3-5 simple action steps.

An Alternative to PowerPoint is to Use a Program Such as Word

- Copy and paste section titles and their corresponding bullet points to blank pages of a Word document.
- Add images and expand on the content & save in PDF format.

Day 14: Develop the Content for Module Three

Welcome to Day 14 of the 30 Day Course Creation Challenge. Today's action step is to create content for module three. You can deliver content in PDF format alone or along with audio content, via a teleseminar call.

Here are some options to chose from:

➤ Add section titles & corresponding bullet points to PowerPoint slides.

➤ Or copy and paste section titles and their corresponding bullet points into a Word document and save in PDF format.

➤ From there, you can add images and/or additional content as needed.

Turn to *Today's Journal Page* and title this module's section concepts.

Notes and Ideas

_____

_____

_____

_____

_____

_____

_____

_____

_____

_____

Today's Journal Page
Develop the Content for Module #___

List the Key Concepts You'd Like to Teach in This Module.

Turn back to the outline you created for this module and transfer the key concepts you listed, in the spaces below.

○ _____

○ _____

○ _____

○ _____

Compose Section Titles for This Module

Now transform those concepts into benefit driven section titles. Focus on what students will gain by going through each section.

○ _____

○ _____

○ _____

○ _____

Tips for Expanding Section Titles into Course Content

Turn the page for additional exercises to help you develop the content for your course modules. The easiest way to create course content is to:

- Transfer your section titles and bullet points to PowerPoint slides or to blank pages of a Word document.

- You can then add images and expand the content from there.

Action Page for Day 14

Develop Course Content for Module #___

In the spaces below, list your module *Section Titles* for this module, from the previous page. Then compose a list of bullet points you'll cover in each of these sections. You can transfer this content to PowerPoint slides or add each section to a blank page of a Word document and expand the content from there.

Section Title: _____

- O _____
- O _____
- O _____

Section Title: _____

- O _____
- O _____
- O _____

Section Title: _____

- O _____
- O _____
- O _____

Section Title: _____

- O _____
- O _____
- O _____

Create Course Content Using PowerPoint Slides

PowerPoint is a fantastic tool for creating your course content. It is simple to use and it is easy to add text and images. PowerPoint slides, saved in PDF format, can stand alone as module content, or can complement a tele-seminar type conference call.

Tips for Creating PowerPoint Slides for Your Modules

➤ You never want to give students your PowerPoint slides. Instead, you can save 3 slides to a page with room for notes, and save as a PDF file.

➤ When creating slides, realize that less is more and images are great.

➤ Use minimal text and add no more than 3-4 bullets per slide.

➤ Make sure your text is visible by using 28-32 point font.

➤ Add images as this will keep your audience engaged. Make sure you have the rights to use these images. You can purchase them for about a dollar each at places like Fotolia.com and you can get them for free at public domain websites such as Pixabay.com

Suggestions for Which Slides to Include in Your Module

- Welcome to (Course Name) - The focus of today's module is...
- What We'll Cover in this Module. Add bullet points.
- Section Title Slides. Add a section title slide for each section of the module. On these slides list the bullet points from the previous page.
- You can then add 1-3 slides after each section title slide, and fill in the content (text and images) from there.
- Time to Take Action. Provide students with 3-5 simple action steps.

An Alternative to PowerPoint is to Use a Program Such as Word

- Copy and paste section titles and their corresponding bullet points to blank pages of a Word document.
- Add images and expand on the content & save in PDF format.

Day 15: Develop the Content for Module Four

Welcome to Day 15 of the 30 Day Course Creation Challenge. Today's action step is to create content for module four. You can deliver content in PDF format alone or along with audio content, via a teleseminar call.

Here are some options to chose from:

➤ Add section titles & corresponding bullet points to PowerPoint slides.

➤ Or copy and paste section titles and their corresponding bullet points into a Word document and save in PDF format.

➤ From there, you can add images and/or additional content as needed.

Turn to *Today's Journal Page* and title this module's section concepts.

Note: Skip ahead to locate the *Course Content Master for Additional Modules*.

Notes and Ideas

_____

_____

_____

_____

_____

_____

_____

_____

_____

Today's Journal Page
Develop the Content for Module #___

List the Key Concepts You'd Like to Teach in This Module.

Turn back to the outline you created for this module and transfer the key concepts you listed, in the spaces below.

O _____

O _____

O _____

O _____

Compose Section Titles for This Module

Now transform those concepts into benefit driven section titles. Focus on what students will gain by going through each section.

O _____

O _____

O _____

O _____

Tips for Expanding Section Titles into Course Content

Turn the page for additional exercises to help you develop the content for your course modules. The easiest way to create course content is to:

- Transfer your section titles and bullet points to PowerPoint slides or to blank pages of a Word document.

- You can then add images and expand the content from there.

Action Page for Day 15

Develop Course Content for Module #____

In the spaces below, list your module *Section Titles* for this module, from the previous page. Then compose a list of bullet points you'll cover in each of these sections. You can transfer this content to PowerPoint slides or add each section to a blank page of a Word document and expand the content from there.

Section Title: _____

- ○ _____
- ○ _____
- ○ _____

Section Title: _____

- ○ _____
- ○ _____
- ○ _____

Section Title: _____

- ○ _____
- ○ _____
- ○ _____

Section Title: _____

- ○ _____
- ○ _____
- ○ _____

Create Course Content Using PowerPoint Slides

PowerPoint is a fantastic tool for creating your course content. It is simple to use and it is easy to add text and images. PowerPoint slides, saved in PDF format, can stand alone as module content, or can complement a tele-seminar type conference call.

Tips for Creating PowerPoint Slides for Your Modules

> ➤ You never want to give students your PowerPoint slides. Instead, you can save 3 slides to a page with room for notes, and save as a PDF file.

> ➤ When creating slides, realize that less is more and images are great.

> ➤ Use minimal text and add no more than 3-4 bullets per slide.

> ➤ Make sure your text is visible by using 28-32 point font.

> ➤ Add images as this will keep your audience engaged. Make sure you have the rights to use these images. You can purchase them for about a dollar each at places like Fotolia.com and you can get them for free at public domain websites such as Pixabay.com

Suggestions for Which Slides to Include in Your Module

- Welcome to (Course Name) - The focus of today's module is...
- What We'll Cover in this Module. Add bullet points.
- Section Title Slides. Add a section title slide for each section of the module. On these slides list the bullet points from the previous page.
- You can then add 1-3 slides after each section title slide, and fill in the content (text and images) from there.
- Time to Take Action. Provide students with 3-5 simple action steps.

An Alternative to PowerPoint is to Use a Program Such as Word

- Copy and paste section titles and their corresponding bullet points to blank pages of a Word document.
- Add images and expand on the content & save in PDF format.

Course Content Master for Additional Modules: Module #___
Make a copy of this page for each additional module in your course.

In the spaces below, list your module *Section Titles* for this module. Then compose a list of bullet points you'll cover in each of these sections. You can transfer this content to PowerPoint slides or add each section to a blank page of a Word document and expand the content from there.

Section Title: _____

- O _____
- O _____
- O _____

Section Title: _____

- O _____
- O _____
- O _____

Section Title: _____

- O _____
- O _____
- O _____

Section Title: _____

- O _____
- O _____
- O _____

Course Content Master for Additional Modules: Module #____
Make a copy of this page for each additional module in your course.

In the spaces below, list your module *Section Titles* for this module. Then compose a list of bullet points you'll cover in each of these sections. You can transfer this content to PowerPoint slides or add each section to a blank page of a Word document and expand the content from there.

Section Title: _____

- ○ _____
- ○ _____
- ○ _____

Section Title: _____

- ○ _____
- ○ _____
- ○ _____

Section Title: _____

- ○ _____
- ○ _____
- ○ _____

Section Title: _____

- ○ _____
- ○ _____
- ○ _____

Day 16: Create Course Support Materials

Welcome to Day 16 of the 30 Day Course Creation Challenge. Today's action step is to create support materials for your course modules.

Go through your course content and get clear on what you want your students to walk away with at the end of each module. Choose the top 3 things you'd like them to take action on. Next, develop support materials, such as action pages, checklists, and worksheets, to help them track their activity and their results.

Turn to *Today's Journal Page* and begin to map out a plan for the type of action pages and support materials you'll create.

Notes and Realizations

_____

_____

_____

_____

_____

_____

_____

_____

_____

_____

_____

Today's Journal Page
Create Course Support Materials & Action Pages

Now that you've created your course content, this is a great time to go through each module and create support materials for your students.

Here are some ideas and suggestions to get you started:

☐ Checklists, quetionnaires, and worksheets make great action pages.

☐ Look back through the action pages for this course to help stimulate ideas for types of action pages you can create.

☐ Provide a way for your students to recap and capture what they learn in each module of your course.

What kind of support materials do you want to create for your course? Jot down your thoughts and ideas in the space below.

Thoughts and Ideas

Turn the page and map out a plan, for the type of support materials and action pages you'll create for your students. If your course will be more than four modules long, make copies of the following pages.

Action Page for Day 16

What Action Steps Do You Want Students to Take

In the spaces below, list the module numbers and titles along with three action steps you'd like for your students to take at the end of each module.

Module 1 Title: _____

Action Steps I'd like my students to take after completing this module:

○ _____

○ _____

○ _____

Module 2 Title: _____

Action Steps I'd like my students to take after completing this module:

○ _____

○ _____

○ _____

Module 3 Title: _____

Action Steps I'd like my students to take after completing this module:

○ _____

○ _____

○ _____

Module 4 Title: _____

Action Steps I'd like my students to take after completing this module:

○ _____

○ _____

○ _____

Jot Down Your Notes and Ideas for the Type of Support Materials You'll Create

Each module is unique, so your support materials will vary. You may find it helpful to develop the materials, one module at a time, as you go through and review each module of your course.

Module One

_____

_____

_____

_____

_____

Module Two

_____

_____

_____

_____

_____

Module Three

_____

_____

_____

_____

Module Four

_____

_____

_____

_____

Notes

Welcome To...

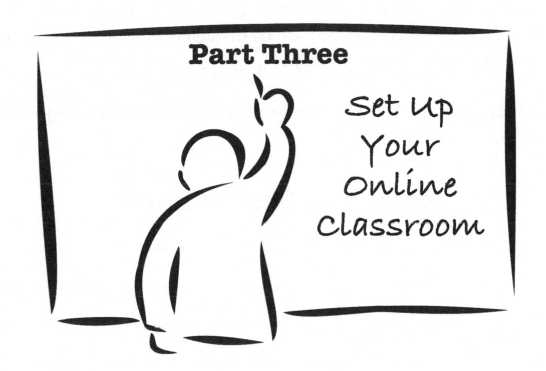

Part Three

Set Up
Your
Online
Classroom

Day 17: Decide on Course Delivery Schedule

Welcome to Day 17 of the 30 Day Course Creation Challenge. Today's action step is to decide on your course delivery schedule.

Once you decide on your course delivery schedule you can begin to prepare your content for delivery. Will your course be delivered one or more times a week, once a week, once a month, daily for 30 days, or...? Once you've decided when your content will be delivered, you can begin to prepare your course content for delivery.

Turn to *Today's Journal Page* and do some brainstorming regarding your course delivery schedule.

Notes and Realizations

_____

_____

_____

_____

_____

_____

_____

_____

_____

_____

Today's Journal Page
My Course Delivery Schedule

Once you decide on your course schedule
you can begin to prepare your content for delivery.

How often will your course content be delivered:

☐ Once a week

☐ One or more times a week for one or more weeks

☐ Several sessions a day for one or more days

☐ Once a month

☐ Daily for 30 Days

☐ Other: _____

_____

Once you've decided on your delivery schedule, you can prepare your course content for delivery. Here are some popular options:

○ Live or recorded audio modules with Q&A

➤ www.FreeConferenceCalling.com

➤ www.WebTeleseminars.com

○ Live or recorded webinars with Q&A

➤ www.GoToMeeting.com

➤ www.WebTeleseminars.com

○ Monthly workshop series with Q&A

➤ Like our Insider's Club: ReachMoreReaders.com/insiders

○ Daily, over the course of 30 Days

➤ Like our 30 Day Challenges: ReachMoreReaders.com/learn

Action Page for Day 17

67

Day 18: Set Up Your Online Classroom

Welcome to Day 18 of the 30 Day Course Creation Challenge. Today's action step is to set up your online classroom. Your online classroom provides you with a secure way to deliver your course content. There are many online options available to choose from. The two most popular options are:

➤ A WordPress plugin, such as *Wishlist Member*, which allows you to set up your classroom, and accept payments, from your website. (This option is more complicated and involved.)

➤ An online classroom platform, such as *Thinkific*, which provides you with a turnkey solution for setting up your course quickly and easily. (This option is an easy way to get an online classroom up and running.)

Turn to *Today's Journal Page* and get started setting up your classroom.

Notes and Realizations

_____

_____

_____

_____

_____

_____

_____

_____

_____

_____

Today's Journal Page
Set Up Your Online Classroom

While there are a lot of options available on the market, the classroom platform I recommend is called Thinkific. Thinkific offers you a turnkey solution and makes it possible for you to set up your classroom, quickly and easily.

Here are a few of the features available to you at Thinkific

- Get your own online classroom, hosted on their website
- Easily upload audio, video, and PDF content
- Accept payments from your students
- Have your own affiate program, so you can offer a commission to people who refer new students to your course
- Connect your email program to your classroom, so you can grow your list of email subscribers and communicate with students.
- Offer quizzes and surveys to your students
- Access a handy and efficient way for you to share your brilliance

Tips for Setting Up Your Classroom at Thinkific.com

- ➤ Register for a free or basic acccount
- ➤ Select a name for your classroom. Since you have the ability to add more than one course to your classroom, you may want to select a classroom name, based on your brand or your overall message
- ➤ Register for their weekly tutorials as you'll learn a great deal
- ➤ Scroll through their tutorials and make the most of their training
- ➤ Locate their support desk is as they are great at answering questions

Action Page for Day 18

Day 19: Upload Your Course Content

Welcome to Day 19 of the 30 Day Course Creation Challenge. Today's action step is to upload your course content to your online classroom.

At this point, you may or may not have created all of the content for every module of your course, that's okay. What you can do is map out a plan and schedule time in your calendar, to create the content for each of the modules of your course.

Turn to *Today's Journal Page* and follow the steps for uploading your course content to your online classroom. Regardless of how many modules you've completed, your task for this action step is to finish creating the content for module one and then upload it to your online classroom.

Notes and Realizations

_____

_____

_____

_____

_____

_____

_____

_____

_____

_____

Today's Journal Page
Upload Your Course Content to Your Classroom

As you continue to create the content for your course, focus on completing one module at a time. This will provide you with a sense of accomplishment and allow you to build on a solid foundation. Once you have your first module created, you can begin uploading course content to your online classroom. Your online classroom is where your students go to access all of the content for your course.

Uploading your content to your online classroom:

☐ The online classroom platform I'm using for my course is: _____

☐ Login to your online classroom and look for the tutorials section. Each online classroom platform has it's own set of training as well as access to their support desk.

☐ Once you are familiar with the process for uploading course content, upload module one of your course to your online classroom. By focusing on uploading one module at a time, you can make sure everything is in order before moving on to the uploading of the next module.

☐ Many online classroom platforms, such as Thinkific, allow you to drip the content to your students. What this does is provides students with access to one module or section at a time. For example, when a student enrolls, they can receive access to module one. Then seven days later, they receive access to module two. Each student's clock begins on they day they enroll.

What I'm most excited about in regards to having an online classroom:

_____

_____

What it'll mean to me to have paying students who want to learn from me:

_____

_____

Action Page for Day 19

Day 20: Create a Sales Page for Your Course

Welcome to Day 20 of the 30 Day Course Creation Challenge. Today's action step is to create a sales page for your course.

A sales page is where people go to find out about and register for your course. If you use an online classroom, such as Thinkific, you'll have access to a sales page as part of your membership.

If your sales page is on a different platform, you can use a blank webpage or a WordPress landing page plugin such as Thrive Themes Content Builder.

Turn to *Today's Journal Page* and map out a plan for your sales page.

Notes and Realizations

_____

_____

_____

_____

_____

_____

_____

_____

_____

_____

Today's Journal Page
Create a Sales Page Outline for Your Course

Your sales page provides a way for people to find out about and register for your course. The words written on the page, known as *copy*, should focus on the challenges your students face along with the benefits your program offers.

Anatomy of a Sales Page - Turn the page for a fill-in-the blanks template

☐ Compose a benefit driven title, which goes at the top of the page

☐ Add an emotion provoking subtitle, such as a question, that allows readers to get in touch with their pain

☐ Add a paragraphs that acknowledges the reader's challenge

☐ Paint the picture of how things could be better

☐ Describe what your program can offer them, focusing on how they'll benefit by going thorough your program. (Focus on the benefits to the students and what they'll gain and not what stuff they'll receive.

☐ Include a benefit driven title and a few benefit driven bullet points for each modele in our program. (Example: Rather than saying, you'll learn how to set up your website, say something like: Discover how to create a magnetic book blog, that will keep visitors coming back time after time.

☐ Include testimonials

☐ Add a way for students to pay for their course registration

☐ Decide on Pricing and Set Up Your Buy Button

- If you are registering students through Thinkific (for example) they walk you through how to integrate payment through PayPal.

- If you're selling from your website or landing page, you can set up a "buy" button in PayPal.

Action Page for Day 20

Map Out the Content for Your Sales Page

Compose a benefit driven title, which goes at the top of the page: _____

_____

Add an emotion provoking subtitle, such as a question, that allows readers to get in touch with their pain: _____

_____

Add a paragraph that acknowledges their challenge:_____

_____

_____

_____

Describe what your program can offer your students, focusing on how they'll benefit by going through your program. Focus on the benefits to the students and what they'll gain rather than the "stuff" they'll receive.

_____

_____

_____

Include a benefit driven title and a few benefit driven bullet points for each module in our program. (Example: Rather than saying, you'll learn how to set up your website, say something like: Discover how to create a magnetic book blog, that will keep visitors coming back time after time.)

_____

_____

Map Out the Content for Your Sales Page

Provide a module by module outline of your program. Rather than list the name of the title and the concepts they'll learn, compose text that focuses on the benefits they'll receive from each module. On your sales page, include benefit driven titles and a few benefit driven bullet points for each module in your program.

- Turn back to day 6, where you mapped out your module topic areas, and draw from that content when composing benefit driven bullet points

- Example: Rather than saying, "You'll learn how to set up your website." You could say something like: "Discover how to create a magnetic book blog, that will keep visitors coming back time after time."

Transform your module titles and key concepts into benefit driven statements:

Module: _____

   Benefit: _____

   Benefit: _____

   Benefit: _____

Module: _____

   Benefit: _____

   Benefit: _____

   Benefit: _____

Module: _____

   Benefit: _____

   Benefit: _____

   Benefit: _____

Module: _____

   Benefit: _____

   Benefit: _____

   Benefit: _____

Day 21: Create Course Auto-Responder Series

Welcome to Day 21 of the 30 Day Course Creation Challenge. Today's action step is to create your course auto-responder series.

An auto-responder provides you with a way to schedule emails to go out automatically. This will keep your students engaged while providing them with easy access to the course content.

Compose a series of emails that let course participants know new that content is available. If your content is delivered weekly, for example, you can schedule your auto-responder emails to go out weekly, automatically.

Turn to *Today's Journal Page* and map out your auto-responder series.

Notes and Realizations

_____

_____

_____

_____

_____

_____

_____

_____

_____

_____

Today's Journal Page
Create Your Course Auto-Responder Series

Having a way to easily let your students know that new content is available to them is essential. By automating this process, you are able to streamline your efforts while helping a lot more people to access your content.

There are many auto-responder companies on the Internet today. The most popular option is AWeber (www.WebmailConnections.com) - as they have one of the highest deliverability rates and best customer training & service.

Anatomy of a Course Email Message for Your Auto-Responder Series

Email Subject Line: Choose 1-2 words that you'll use at the beginning of each course message, so your students can easily locate these messages. As an example, we use [Author Challenge] in the subject lines for this course.

Personalized Greeting: Most email service providers, such as AWeber, provide you with a way to personalize your messages by adding your students' names to the subject lines and the body of the messages. This adds a nice touch and increases the odds of recipients opening your email.

Create a consistent formula for your course auto-responder messages so your students know that to expect. Be sure to use white space between paragraphs.

- Welcome students to the new module and let the know the topic.
- Compose a brief paragraph describing what they'll be learning.
- Include an action step right in the body of the email, if applicable.
- Provide them with links to your classroom and the action pages.
- End the email as you would end a letter to a friend, and add your name. (Example: I end my email messages with "Here's to your success, D'vorah."

~.~

Your Action Step: Open a Word document and compose the auto-responder series for your course. Save them in a file on your hard drive for easy access.

Action Page for Day 21

Day 22: Set Up a Course Facebook Group

Welcome to Day 22 of the 30 Day Course Creation Challenge. Today's action step is to create a Facebook Group for your course.

Providing your students with a way to connect with you and with other participants, so they can ask questions and share successes and challenges, can really add value to your program. The easiest way to accomplish this is by setting up a private Facebook discussion group.

Turn to *Today's Journal Page* and follow the steps, as you set up your group. You'll need to provide your students with a link to the group and instruct them to click the "join" button. You can then approve their membership and welcome them to the group.

Notes and Realizations

_____

_____

_____

_____

_____

_____

_____

_____

_____

_____

Today's Journal Page
Creating a Facebook Group for Your Course

Follow the instructions below to set up your Facebook group.

Step One: Login (or set up a profile) at Facebook.com.

Step Two: Scroll to the left or the bottom of the page to locate the "groups" tab. Once you've done this you can click to "create a new group."

Note: In order to set up a group, you first have to add someone to your group. If you are not yet ready to add students, you can add a friend, colleague, or family member, with their permission of course. You can remove them from the group later, if you'd like.

Step Three: Decide on a branded name for your group.

The name for my group will be: _____

Step Four: Adjust group settings, via the settings tab. The setting you'll want to adjust is the one that states whether you want students to be able to automatically add new members, or if you'd like to approve new members. I recommend setting it so you can approve membership.

Step Five: Select a branded URL (web address) for your group. From the settings tab you'll also find the option to create a custom URL for your group. Choose carefully as it is very difficult to have it changed. Select something related to your brand, or to your course (if this group will be exclusive to this course) and make sure it is easy to say and spell.

The URL to my Facebook group is: _____

Step Six: Welcome your students to the group by providing them with the URL and an invitation via email. You can also post a link to your group in your member's area. (You may want to wait until you have a few members before inviting people to join.)

Have fun with your Facebook group! This is a fantastic way for you to get to know your students, and build ongoing relationships with them.

Action Page for Day 22

Day 23: Make Sure All Systems Are Go

Welcome to Day 23 of the 30 Day Course Creation Challenge. Today's action step is to make sure all of your systems in place and test those systems, before inviting students to join your course.

There are many moving parts involved when setting up an online course. Once you are sure that everything is in working order, you'll want to log out of all your accounts and websites, and go through the registration process as if you were a new student. If you find something that needs adjusting, make the adjustment, then logout and try it again.

Turn to *Today's Journal Page* and refer to the 3-2-1 Blastoff Checklist. Congratulations!

Notes and Realizations

_____

_____

_____

_____

_____

_____

_____

_____

_____

_____

Today's Journal Page

3-2-1 Blastoff - Test to Make Sure All Systems Are Go!

It is essential that you test all of your systems to make sure everything is in place, before inviting people to join your program. Refer to the following checklist to help you with this process.

- ☐ Set up your course classroom.
- ☐ Upload the course content content.
- ☐ Set up your course payment processor through PayPal.
- ☐ Set the cost of your course to $1.00 and test your payment processor.
- ☐ Once you test your payment processor, be sure to set the course price back to the regular price.
- ☐ Set up your course auto-responder and connect it to your course.
- ☐ Set up your Facebook group and add a link to the member's area.

Once you have triple checked that everything is set up properly, log out of all your accounts, and test your systems by registering as a test student.

- ○ Make sure all systems are go and the payment processes correctly
- ○ Check to make sure you have access to the course content
- ○ Check to see that you received the automated email for your course

Once all systems are go, begin inviting people to register for your course! Make notes of things you discover through this process. This will help you in the future.

_____

_____

_____

Notes

Welcome To...

Part Four

Market Your Course and Open the Doors

Day 24: Market Your Course via Email

Welcome to Day 24 of the 30 Day Course Creation Challenge. Today's action step is to compose email messages and market your course to your list.

Your email list is comprised of members of your target audience who have indicated that they are interested in what you have to say. Provide valuable and interesting content to your list on your topic area. This will also provide you with the opportunity to promote your course to them. Take care to focus on building relationships and sharing value. Then, when you go to market your course, people will see this as another way to learn from you.

Turn to *Today's Journal Page* and prepare to create educational as well as marketing messages, so you can let your list know about your course.

Notes and Realizations

_____

_____

_____

_____

_____

_____

_____

_____

_____

_____

_____

Today's Journal Page
Preparing Educational and Marketing Messages

Email marketing is a mix of providing education and inspiration along with opportunities for people to invest in resources that support their goals.

Create a set of emails that are designed to educate your subscribers.

- O Use compelling subject lines that will entice your subscribers.

- O Begin your email with a warm welcome or friendly greeting.

- O Tell a short story or share something you recently learned, based on the topic of your email message.

- O Keep paragraphs short and leave white space between paragraphs.

- O Tie in the email message to the topic of to your course.

- O Include an invitation to register for your course.

You'll also want to create a series of email messages that are focused on enrolling people into your course.

- O Turn back to the Day 20 action steps and draw from the content on your sales page, when creating your marketing messages.

- O Include compelling headlines and ask questions that inspire action.

- O Focus on the benefits to the students and what they'll gain rather than the "stuff" they'll receive.

- O Describe what your program can offer your students, focusing on how they'll benefit by going through your course. Then invite them to enroll.

Turn the page and complete the exercises for outlining a series of educational emails as well as a series of promotional emails.

Action Page for Day 24

Crafting Your Email Subject Lines

The most important aspect of an email is the subject line. Your subject line is what determines whether or not people open your emails. When composing email subject lines, use words that will intrigue your readers.

Create a list of topics you could write about, related to your online course:

_____

_____

_____

_____

_____

Transform this informative list of topics into compelling email subject lines:

_____

_____

_____

_____

You'll also want to create subject lines that directly promote your course:

_____

_____

_____

_____

_____

Create an Outline with Ideas for Your Emails

Use the space below to brainstorm ideas for your educational emails and your marketing emails. Then, open up a Word document, compose your messages, and save them to your computer.

Hot Tip: Always reread what you've composed, putting yourself in the shoes of your subscribers, before sending out an email.

Notes for Email Message #1

_____

_____

_____

_____

_____

_____

Notes for Email Message #2

_____

_____

_____

_____

_____

_____

Notes for Email Message #3

_____

_____

_____

_____

_____

Notes for Email Message #4

_____

_____

_____

_____

_____

Day 25: Market Course via Guest Blogging

Welcome to Day 25 of the 30 Day Course Creation Challenge. Today's action step is to pave the way towards marketing your course via guest blogging.

Guest blogging is where you participate as a guest author on the blogs that attract your target audience. By featuring you as a guest blogger, blog owners will be endorsing you and introducing you to their audiences.

Turn to *Today's Journal Page* and map out a plan for locating and writing for blogs in your niche. By writing for blogs that attract your ideal readers, you will have the opportunity to share content with people who are interested in your topic. This audience is also likely to be interested in your course.

Notes and Realizations

_____

_____

_____

_____

_____

_____

_____

_____

_____

_____

Today's Journal Page
Prepare to Become a Guest Blogger

As a guest blogger, it is essential that you locate and write articles for blogs that attract your ideal readers.

Compose a list of topics your target audience is interested in, related to your expertise and the topic of your course.

- ○ _____
- ○ _____
- ○ _____
- ○ _____
- ○ _____

Create a list of blogs, in your niche, that you'd like to write for.

- List the blogs of your colleagues and leaders in your field.
- Look for guest bloggers on those blogs. Add their blogs to your list.
- Go to www.BlogSearchEngine.org. Search for blogs on your topic.

Blog Owner's Name	Topic of Blog	Blog's Website Address
_____	_____	_____
_____	_____	_____
_____	_____	_____
_____	_____	_____
_____	_____	_____
_____	_____	_____
_____	_____	_____

Action Page for Day 25

Map Out Ideas for Your Blog Posts

Blog posts are typically 450-850 words in length. Each blog owner sets the standard for their blog, so be sure to ask how long your posts should be. Map out your ideas and initial outlines for your blog posts.

Outline for Post #1

_____

_____

_____

_____

_____

_____

_____

_____

_____

_____

_____

_____

_____

_____

Outline for Post #2

_____

_____

_____

_____

_____

_____

_____

_____

_____

_____

_____

_____

_____

_____

Create a Signature for Your Blog Posts

It is customary to include a 100-150 word signature section at the end of each of your posts. For maximum benefit, let readers know that they can receive a free gift (such as a checklist or top tips list) by going to your web-site. This will allow you to grow your email list. In your signature you can also include a short link to your book over on Amazon.

Compose your blog signature and copy it to a Word document, where you can save it to your computer hard drive for easy access.

_____

_____

_____

_____

_____

Outline for Post #3

_____

_____

_____

_____

_____

_____

_____

_____

_____

Outline for Post #4

_____

_____

_____

_____

_____

_____

_____

_____

_____

Day 26: Market Course via Guest Speaking

Welcome to Day 26 of the 30 Day Course Creation Challenge. Today's action step is to locate online speaking opportunities, where you can share your message with listeners who are keenly interested in your topic area.

A powerful way to form a connection with your audience is to provide them with opportunities to hear your voice and your passion for your topic.

Turn to *Today's Journal Page* and identify potential speaking opportunities. Make it a priority to focus on speaking to audiences who are interested in your topic area. This will increase your credibility and get you in front of listeners who could be interested in your course.

Notes and Realizations

_____

_____

_____

_____

_____

_____

_____

_____

_____

_____

Today's Journal Page
Locating Online Speaking Opportunities

The easiest way to get started with online speaking is to interview and get interviewed by people you already know, who attract members of your target audience. Once the interview has concluded, be sure to thank your hosts and ask them for referrals to others who interview, in your niche.

Name of Host	Name of Show or Podcast	Website Address

To locate additional online speaking opportunities go to iTunes and BlogTalkRadio.com and search for hosts and shows on your topic area.

Name of Host	Name of Show or Podcast	Website Address

Action Page for Day 26

Compose a List of Interview Questions

While some hosts prepare a set of questions to ask during interviews, most will request a list of possible questions, from their guests. This allows guests to prepare and focus on topics they are familiar with. For a half-hour interview, you'll typically need 5-7 questions. For an hour long interview, provide 10-12 questions. Practice answering these questions beforehand.

Here's a sample list of questions you can add to or draw from:

○ Tell us about your success journey.

○ How did you come to write your book?

○ Can you please share a brief synopsis of your book?

○ How did you get interested in this topic area?

○ Could you please share 3 top tips from your book?

○ Additional question: _____

○ Additional question: _____

○ Additional question: _____

○ What is one thing our listeners can do, in the next 24 hours, to take action on what they learned during this interview?

○ Which website should people go to to find out more about you?

○ What thoughts would you like to leave our listeners with?

Compose alternate questions below. Choose 8-10 total to send to hosts.

○ _____

○ _____

○ _____

○ _____

94 Open up a Word document and compose your master list of interview questions. Save these to a folder on your hard drive.

Craft Your Speaker Bio

Use the following template to compose your speaker bio. This is what your hosts will read when introducing you to their listeners. Strive to keep your bio under 100 words, unless your host indicates otherwise. This way you'll focus on what's essential and will retain the attention of your listeners.

(Name)_____ of (URL) www._____

is the (author of or expert on): _____.

(One sentence that describe your experience) _____

_____

(One sentence that describes what "you do" or how you help people) _____

_____.

Today (name) will be speaking to us about: _____.

Draw from the above outline to compose your speaker bio: _____

_____

_____

_____

_____

Hot Tip: Typically, at the end of an interview, the host will ask you to let people know the best way to get in touch with you. Rather than giving your listeners multiple options, give them one URL so they take action.

The most effective option is to let them know that you have a special gift for them, which they can receive by going to your website. Provide them with the URL to where they go to register their name and email address in exchange for your gift. This will get them onto your email list.

You'll then have the opportunity to build ongoing relationships as well as market your course.

Day 27: Market via the Social Networks

Welcome to Day 27 of the 30 Day Course Creation Challenge. Today's action step is to find ways to market your course via the social networks.

While you don't want to appear "salesy" there are many ways you can gently share your message and promote your course via the social networks. Focus on sharing knowledge and inspiration, and answering questions, as this will set you apart while demonstrating your expertise. This will also present you with opportunities to mention your course and invite people to participate.

Turn to *Today's Journal Page* and outline your social networking plan.

Notes and Realizations

_____

_____

_____

_____

_____

_____

_____

_____

_____

_____

Today's Journal Page
Map Out a Social Networking Plan

The thing about the social networks is, people either avoid them for fear of spending hours floating around on the Internet, or they dive in and end up spending way to much time, doing what could take minutes. The key is to actually schedule times for social networking.

Here is a list of activities you can participate in, in a few short minutes.

- Post inspiring quotes and comments
- Post links to informative blog posts
- Add inspiring quotes and your website address to images
- Participate in conversations
- Answer questions and share your expertise
- Let people know about your course

Create a list of the online groups you participate in, that are related to your area of expertise. Schedule time, at least once a week, to visit those groups. While there, share a brief update or an inspiring quote. Also make it a point to share your thoughts or answer a question, posted by other members.

Social Network	Name of Group	Day & Time You'll Visit
_____	_____	_____
_____	_____	_____
_____	_____	_____

Create a file on interesting or inspiring quotes. You can find great quotes, on just about any topic, at BrainyQuote.com. Jot down a few quotes here:

_____

_____

_____

Action Page for Day 27

Day 28: Develop Joint Venture Relationships

Welcome to Day 28 of the 30 Day Course Creation Challenge. Today's action step is to identify potential joint venture partners.

The ideal joint venture partner, is someone whose audience is similar to yours. Their topic complements yours and this creates an opportunity for you to promote and endorse one another. Joint venture partners can promote one another for no financial gain, however, it is a common practice to offer affiliate commissions when someone refers paying customers to you. There are many online affilite programs to choose from, such as Thinkific, JVZoo, and iDev Affiliate.

Turn to *Today's Journal Page* and identify potential joint venture partners.

Notes and Realizations

_____

_____

_____

_____

_____

_____

_____

_____

_____

_____

Identify Possible Joint Venture Partners

Create a list of people you know and people you know of, who speak or write on topics that would be of interest to your audience. This means that their audience would be interested in what you speak or write about.

When approaching potential joint venture partners, focus on developing a relationship with them and being of support to them. One way to do this is to offer to get them in front of a new audience. Let them know that your audience is very interested in their topic area and that you'd love to feature them as a guest speaker or guest blogger. You can also ask if they host guest speakers, as you are expanding your speaking schedule.

To make it easy for potential hosts to say "yes" create a page on your website where you post links to your guest blog posts and online interviews.

People I know who speak or write on topics of interest to my audience:

○ _____
○ _____
○ _____
○ _____
○ _____

People I do not yet know, but would love to get to know, who speak or write on topics of interest to my audience:

○ _____
○ _____
○ _____
○ _____
○ _____

Action Page for Day 28

Day 29: Open the Doors to Your Classroom

Welcome to Day 29 of the 30 Day Course Creation Challenge. Today's action step is to put a plan in place to be able to open the doors of your classroom.

Schedule time in your calendar to finish creating your course content and developing your sales page and marketing materials. By chipping away at these tasks, you'll have your course completed, and available for purchase, in record time.

Turn to *Today's Journal Page* and work your way through the activities, so you are prepared and able to open the doors to your classroom!

Notes and Realizations

_____

_____

_____

_____

_____

_____

_____

_____

_____

_____

Today's Journal Page
Getting Ready to Open the Doors to My Classroom

Turn back to pages 4-7 to access your "At-A-Glance" action steps. This will provide you with a step-by-step blueprint, of what we covered in this program. Work your way through all 30 steps and you'll be ready to open the doors to your classroom and welcome your new students!

Here are the key components to complete, to bring your course to market:

- ☐ Identify your "why" and your topic and create your course outline
- ☐ Develop your course content and upload it to your classroom
- ☐ Create your sales page and your marketing materials
- ☐ Participate in guest blogging and guest speaking
- ☐ Promote your course and welcome your students

What it'll mean to me to be able to begin enrolling students in my course:

_____

_____

_____

What I need to put in place to be able to focus on completing my course:

_____

_____

_____

Notes: _____

_____

_____

Day 30: Celebration and Next Steps

Welcome to Day 30 of the 30 Day Course Creation Challenge. Today's action step is to celebrate your accomplishments and put a plan in place to keep your momentum going.

Congratulations, you made it! But, the journey doesn't end here. You'll want to put a plan in place to keep your momentum going. Wherever you are on the spectrum, from idea to finished product, you are only a decision away from enrolling your ideal students into your new course.

Turn to *Today's Journal Page* and put your next steps plan in place.

Notes and Realizations

_____

_____

_____

_____

_____

_____

_____

_____

_____

_____

Today's Journal Page
Time to Celebrate & Identify Next Steps

It's time to celebrate your accomplishments! If your course is ready to launch, go for it. If your course is still being developed, schedule time to complete it. Wherever you are on this journey, you are in the perfect place. They key is to keep the momentum going.

What I need to do to keep my momentum moving forward:

○ _____

○ _____

○ _____

What I enjoyed most about this course creation challenge:

○ _____

○ _____

○ _____

What I will do to celebrate my accomplishments:

○ _____

○ _____

○ _____

What my next steps are:

○ _____

○ _____

○ _____

Action Page for Day 30

Notes

Next Steps

_____   _____

_____   _____

_____   _____

_____   _____

_____   _____

_____   _____

_____   _____

_____   _____

_____   _____

_____   _____

_____   _____

Tools and Resources for Me

As you design your cource, keep a running list of tools and resources that can support you on your journey.

Audio Content Creation Resources

FreeConferenceCalling	FreeConferenceCalling.com
Instant Teleseminar	WebTeleseminars.com
BlogTalkRadio	BlogTalkRadio.com

Graphic Design, Images, and Infographic Resources

PicMonkey	PicMonkey.com
Canva	Canva.com
Pixabay	Pixabay.com
Fotolia	Fotolia.com
Presenter Media	PresenterMedia.com

List Building and Landing Page Resources

AWeber	WebmailConnections.com
Thrive Themes	ReachMoreReaders.com/thrive

Online Classroom and Membership Site Resources

Thinkific	ReachMoreReaders.com/thinkific
Wishlist Member	ReachMoreReaders.com/wishlist

Private Label Rights Materials

Coach Glue	BookMarketingMadeEasy.com/coachglue
Easy PLR	BookMarketingMadeEasy.com/easyplr

Survey Resources

Survey Monkey	SurveyMonkey.com
Gravity Forms	BookMarketingMadeEasy.com/gravityforms

Video Creation and Hosting Resources

Camtasia Studio	CamtasiaStudio.com
Jing Project	JingProject.com
Snagit	Snagit.com
YouTube	YouTube.com

Tools For My Students and Clients

As you design your course, keep a running list of tools and resources that can support your students and clients on their journey. Whenever possible, sign up as an affiliate for programs.

Tool: URL:	Is there an affiliate program? __ Yes __No Description:
Tool: URL:	Is there an affiliate program? __ Yes __No Description:
Tool: URL:	Is there an affiliate program? __ Yes __No Description:
Tool: URL:	Is there an affiliate program? __ Yes __No Description:
Tool: URL:	Is there an affiliate program? __ Yes __No Description:
Tool: URL:	Is there an affiliate program? __ Yes __No Description:
Tool: URL:	Is there an affiliate program? __ Yes __No Description:
Tool: URL:	Is there an affiliate program? __ Yes __No Description:
Tool: URL:	Is there an affiliate program? __ Yes __No Description:
Tool: URL:	Is there an affiliate program? __ Yes __No Description:
Tool: URL:	Is there an affiliate program? __ Yes __No Description:
Notes	Notes

About D'vorah

D'vorah Lansky, M.Ed. is the bestselling author of several books including; *Book Marketing Made Easy: Simple Strategies for Selling Your Nonfiction Book* Online.

Since 2006 D'vorah has created more than 25, successful, online programs and has taught and coached thousands of authors across the globe.

D'vorah has spoken on over 500 online teleseminars, podcasts, and radio shows. She specializes in teaching authors how to reach more readers and sell more books, using online book marketing strategies.

Also by D'vorah
30 Day Productivity Challenge for Authors

In the 30 Day Productivity Challenge for Authors, you have in your hands a step-by-step guide to productivity. By applying what you learn, in a few short minutes a day, you will become more productive!

Get your copy of this interacctive action guide today, and go from overwhelmed to becoming more productive than you ever believed possible!

$19.95
Available on Amazon.com or a bookstore near you!
ISBN: 978-0996743112

Book Marketing Made Easy: Simple Strategies for Selling Your Nonfiction Book Online

Discover the secrets that successful authors use to market their books on-line. In *Book Marketing Made Easy* you will learn how to: increase your credibility and be seen as an expert in your field; sell more books to people who will benefit from your message; create multiple sources of income with the content of your book; harness the power of multimedia marketing to reach more people; and use social media to increase your influence and expand your market.

$14.95
Available on Amazon.com or a bookstore near you!
ISBN: 978-096519759

CPSIA information can be obtained
at www.ICGtesting.com
Printed in the USA
BVOW07s0822070317
477959BV00003B/42/P